rough
ement

Office of Government Commerce

London: TSO

First published 2002

ISBN 0 11 330898 1

OGC – the Office of Government Commerce – is an office of HM Treasury. Set up in 2000, it incorporates the Central Computer and Telecommunications Agency (CCTA), which no longer operates as a separate agency.

The OGC is now the authority for best practice in commercial activities in UK Government, combining a number of separate functions with related aims.

OGC will build on the popular guidance developed by the former CCTA and others, working with organisations internationally to develop and share business and practitioner guidance within a world-class best practice framework.

Printed in the United Kingdom by The Stationery Office

77969   C20   6/02

CONTENTS

ACKNOWLEDGEMENTS

The Stationery Office, on behalf of OGC, acknowledges with thanks the contribution of material and input for this publication made by David Greenly of Red Door Consulting.

1
INTRODUCTION

Successful organisations need to be able to embrace change.

Experience shows that using a formal project management approach is the most effective way to deliver change well. This book presents the arguments to support that assertion. It describes and recommends the adoption of the PRINCE2 method to provide an organisation with a fast track to successful project management and the business benefits that will follow. A proven project management approach, PRINCE2 (Projects IN Controlled Environments) is described in terms of its generic features with a focus on the benefits these provide to the top team.

Projects are the key enabler for transforming business aspirations (strategy) into manageable actions (changes), which deliver tangible business results (benefits). Although an organisation will take benefit from improving the level of control surrounding change, the step-change in performance will only follow where the disciplines of a Project Environment are integrated into the strategy planning and delivery processes too. Understanding the organisation's project capability provides senior management with an invaluable tool for testing the feasibility of the strategy: there is little value in developing ambitious plans if there is not a delivery mechanism available to achieve them. For many organisations the realisation of business benefits from project management will require a significant cultural shift from the random 'hit and miss' approach, to one that demands more control and discipline, from the top of the organisation to the operational level. To succeed, the cultural transition must be rooted in the very heart of the business and project management nurtured to grow into a core capability of the organisation. This will only happen if there is ownership and determined leadership from the most senior managers. The upside of this for senior management is that PRINCE2 provides a framework within which they can confidently delegate the planning and execution of change with a greatly increased probability of success by ensuring

1

- clarity of purpose, where the objectives of the project are clearly understood by mapping them against the big picture of where the organisation is going
- credible planning, where the implementation of strategy is tested by looking at the project capability and capacity available to manage the changes required
- commitment, where buy-in is achieved from all areas of the organisation through effective communication processes
- control, where projects are planned and delivered in phases allowing for important review points.

Case study 1.1 summarises the experiences of an organisation that transformed itself from an 'also ran' to the leader in its industry. Key to this was the early recognition that a revolution in working practices for the management of change was required, covering the whole corporate planning process. This revolution was driven by the top manager and included the rapid mobilisation of a Project Environment. This capability has been honed and developed over a number of years and has provided the company with a key competitive advantage that has allowed it to sustain its market leading position.

Case study 1.1

A major financial services organisation experienced dramatic increases in business following the deregulation of the personal pensions market. However, the organisation could not cope with the increase and as a result orders were processed poorly. Customers and brokers became disillusioned and withdrew business from the company. The company was ranked as nineteenth out of 20 in broker satisfaction surveys and had a poor reputation in the industry. The company was firmly rooted on a 'burning platform' and needed to take radical action if it was to survive.

A new leader was appointed who set about the task of transforming the organisation. Over a period of time the organisation successfully transformed and rose from nineteenth in the satisfaction survey to first and won a coveted 'Company of the Year' award. One of the key drivers for the turnaround was the recognition for the need and development of a project culture to manage the changes that had to be undertaken. The most senior manager personally championed the development of this capability. The organisation continues to thrive and has retained its market leading position built on the back of its ability to manage change in a controlled and timely way.

2
THE CHANGE IMPERATIVE

Managing change continues to present executives with greater challenges than ever before. Many organisations struggle with the impact of change and find that their plans fail to materialise into benefits. Often organisations see that their carefully planned change is suddenly invalidated by an unforeseen event because their approach to change management is too inflexible to allow them to respond in a timely way.

> **Case study 2.1 An example of poor change control**
>
> An insurance company in the US conducted a 30-person project that took three years to complete, against an original estimate of one year. When it finished, they found that the company had stopped selling the product more than a year before.

The probability of having to make 'emergency' or contingency plans is reduced where the original plan is undertaken in a considered, structured and controlled way.

2.1 Why does change still fail?

Alarmingly, and despite the warnings and lessons learned, up to 80 per cent of all changes fail to deliver the planned benefits. Many run over time and cost and the deliverable does not match the business specification or meet management expectations. Often, the true cost of the change is not evident until the full consequences of the poor delivery are understood.

There are many reasons for failure but broadly speaking changes fail for management reasons rather than technical ones. One of the key

> **Case study 2.2 An example of poor benefits realisation**
>
> A Scandinavian country conducted a survey into the cost-benefit analysis of projects across most of its Government and found that only 16 per cent could document quantitative benefits from investments in change during the previous four years.

management failings is the sloppy approach that some organisations take to managing change.

Ad hoc approaches rarely provide the tight structured environment required for the effective initiation and control of change.

A key issue associated with an ad hoc approach is that a clear business justification for change may never be developed. Rather than change being determined by a formal cost-benefit business appraisal it is often the case that change is driven by a senior personality as opposed to a professional management process. Moreover the change may be insulated within a particular function, isolating other parts of the business from the change and the potential implications of the delivery. The full implications for the whole organisation are sometimes understood only when it is too late and the benefits realised in one part of the business are reduced or even disappear, as an unforeseen negative impact of the change becomes apparent elsewhere.

2.2 The need to control change

Successful organisations have recognised the need to face up to change and be in control of it, rather than let change manage them. Change provides an opportunity to improve the status quo and deliver business benefits as a result.

Improving the status quo requires the definition and delivery of a set of unique outcomes that, once applied to the existing operation, will deliver the necessary improvement in performance. Changes to the status quo will almost certainly cut across functions within the organisation, a fact which has traditionally led to problems of ownership of the changes and consequently difficulty in realising the expected benefits. Improving cross-functional 'team working' requires a new management capability built on the foundation of a controlled and professional environment. The new capability needs to bring together the various parts of the business and focus this collective strength on working together towards a common goal. Successful organisations tend to have adopted a project-based approach. The key characteristics of a PRINCE2 project-based approach are

- Each change has a clear business case
- Clarity of ownership, responsibility and decision making
- Focus on project outcomes rather than activity
- Planning as a core discipline
- Clear definition of scope and benefits at the outset and their continual review
- Buy-in from key stakeholders throughout the life of the project
- Effective cross-functional working
- Principle of a 'customer' and 'supplier' relationship
- Low management overhead through management by exception whilst allowing high levels of control
- Chunking of the project into manageable pieces with control points at the completion of each chunk to test the ongoing justification for the project
- Appropriate attitude to the management of risk and issues
- End user involvement to ensure realistic definition and realisation of project benefits
- Clear communication and reporting structures to drive effective decision making
- Quality defined as 'fitness for purpose' rather than an abstract concept
- Fully supported through accredited trainers and consultants
- Allows learning from experiences, both good and bad, for the ongoing development of project best practice
- No 'routine bureaucracy'.

2.3 How to control change

Where change is managed through a multi-functional team, led by a professional project manager, it is a matter of fact that the chances of success are greatly improved.

5

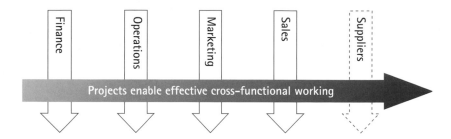

Figure 2.1 The project model is key for effective management

The chances of success are improved still further where the team uses a tried and tested approach to project management. This reduces the overhead for the start-up of each project and provides a framework for building associated skills and giving the senior management the information they require to control the project.

Am I controlling change? A simple health check

With some organisations spending the equivalent of up to 25 per cent of their annual operating budget on projects, it is vital that senior management are able to answer the following questions on a regular basis to determine if there are appropriate controls around the changes:

- What is the budget for projects?
- How many projects are running or planned?
- What is the current status?
- What are the precise benefits that will be delivered?
- What actual benefits have been delivered?
- Who is accountable for realising benefits?
- What are the processes for initiation and control?
- Do we have the skills to deliver the projects, now and in the future?
- Do we have the capacity to accommodate the number of changes?

Senior management need an effective mechanism to allow them to direct the resources of the organisation at the right targets. A well-applied project management approach provides the controlled environment that will allow senior management to initiate projects confidently and delegate some responsibility and authority for their management. Table 2.1 identifies some situations where change should be managed as a project.

Table 2.1 Situations where change could be managed as a project

Situation	Why
Where there is complexity	Coordinates activity and design across a number of functions
Where there is conflict	Ensures that each change is business-justified which in turn drives resource allocation decisions
Where there is the potential for common activity or deliverables	Provides a mechanism for the identification of commonality across the whole
Where there is a probability of change during the project	Processes provide a timely and accurate flow of information to enable effective adjustments to be made
Where there is high risk	Risk management processes ensure that risks are identified, and effective mitigating plans are initiated and tracked

The PRINCE2 method also allows senior management to define the parameters within which the project can operate. Senior management need only be aware when the agreed tolerances are breached. This exception-based reporting allows them to stay close to what is happening but at the same time provides enough freedom for the project to flex in response to the inevitable minor changes that occur. PRINCE2's approach allows for a number of decision points at critical stages in the life of the project, reinforcing the confidence of the senior management, since the initial basis for the investment will come under periodic review against a range of relevant criteria.

2.4 PRINCE2 – an introduction

PRINCE2 is an example of a structured project management approach. It provides a set of best practice processes and is widely used within both the public and private sectors for the effective selection and management of projects. In fact it is the recommended approach within the UK Government who developed it from studies of industrial best practice. Training, consultancy support and support tools for users of PRINCE2 are delivered via an extensive range of accredited suppliers.

PRINCE2 best practice processes are based on other existing project management methods and the lessons from dozens of case studies, as well as consultation with over 150 users. The diversity of organisations involved in developing the best practice processes means that PRINCE2 is highly adaptable to different project circumstances across a broad span of industries and sectors.

Thus, adopting PRINCE2 allows an organisation to avoid the pitfalls of trial and error and gain a fast track to effective project management and the benefits that come from managing change well.

Because the effective management of change is critical for survival and growth it is not enough to take a few good people from the operation and call them project managers; they need to be trained for the task. To encourage and facilitate its use, PRINCE2 is fully supported by a training, accreditation and professional development structure.

PRINCE2's approach calls for a clear business case for every project and checks the validity of that business case at key progress points throughout the project's life. This facilitates the decision making process and allows prioritisation of projects as there is a common means for comparing costs and benefits across candidate projects. The organisation can give appropriate consideration to the deployment of resources and be confident that these resources address the changes that will deliver the greatest return. A measure of an organisation mastering change is that it will have two project lists: one describing and prioritising the projects that it will progress along with the business case for each; the other describing projects that will not be progressed and stating why.

PRINCE2 ensures that many of the issues normally associated with an ad hoc approach to change management are avoided. Table 2.2 highlights some of the key features and the associated benefits of primary importance to senior management:

Table 2.2 The benefits of PRINCE2 to senior management

PRINCE2 Feature	Benefit
Business case	• The project is justified through the development of a clear business case. This describes, at the outset, what the benefits are, the cost and time to produce them, and why it is worth undertaking the project
Clear ownership	• A clear organisation structure is defined which ensures that all parties involved in the project understand roles, responsibilities and who has accountability for delivery of the benefits
Cross-functional working	• Outcome-based focus allows the identification and scheduling of specific skills and activity
Controlled environment	• A phased approach to the project provides a number of critical control points for management. A review takes place at the end of each phase and ensures that the justification for the project is still valid
	• Exception-based management allows senior management to delegate with confidence. Senior management can take the big picture view of the project and need only get involved when agreed tolerances are exceeded
	• Chunking the project up into manageable pieces allows management to commit to one stage at a time. This allows the justification for the project to be periodically reviewed at the end of each stage

Summary

- An organisation needs the ability to manage change well as a key driver for organisational success
- Change requires careful and skilful control
- Project management provides the controlled environment required
- PRINCE2 is a widely used and proven approach and can provide a fast track to project management competence. The key features are that
  - a common language is used which drives understanding and reduces confusion
  - business changes are justified allowing effective resource prioritisation and identification of business benefits
  - the approach is flexible and adaptable to suit organisational preferences
  - low management overhead through exception-based management
  - the process is repeatable so the knowledge from successful projects will grow and become an asset
  - project start-up and execution is reduced as experience develops
  - PRINCE2 projects focus on outcomes rather than activity
  - planning is pragmatic and focuses on a chunk at a time
  - the ongoing justification for the project is reviewed at key points, usually at the end of a chunk
  - proven approach with extensive support network facilitates success
  - project staff morale improves as projects have status, and professional training and accreditation are encouraged and recognised.
- Senior managers must take a lead role. They must embrace change as an opportunity to drive performance. They must achieve this by becoming the active champions of the **Project Environment.**

Chapter 3, *Realising the big picture*, looks at the key role projects play in effective Strategy Definition and Implementation.

3
REALISING THE BIG PICTURE

3.1 Introduction

Having noted that an effective change capability is critical to the organisation's survival and future success, this section demonstrates why a reliable Project Environment is central to the successful translation of strategy into operational changes.

By looking at strategic change empirically, the context and argument for PRINCE2 and how to deploy it effectively can clearly be seen. Too often organisations attempt to 'bolt on' some new capability where it is either inappropriate or where the fundamental conditions for it to operate successfully do not exist.

3.2 Defining and implementing strategy

Organisations need to anticipate and deliver the future needs of their stakeholders and clients (as opposed to constantly being in reactive mode as the environment around them changes). The key capabilities are:

3.2.1 Strategy Definition

- Insight into the future opportunities and threats in the environment in which the organisation operates
- The ability to anticipate the needs and expectations of an organisation's stakeholders and clients in this future state
- The ability to crystallise the organisation's response as a linked set of strategic objectives, critical success factors and strategic Key Performance Indicators (KPIs)
- The ability to define innovative yet achievable future propositions which will deliver value to stakeholders, clients and partners

- The ability to plan an achievable set of actions to deliver the strategy.

3.2.2 Strategy Implementation

- The ability to align operations and projects with strategic objectives
- The ability to initiate the right set of strategic projects
- The discipline to keep projects and operations aligned and to realise the expected benefits.

Having only one of these capabilities is not enough. A winning strategy will not benefit an organisation that is incapable of translating it into meaningful action. On the other hand, being able to implement the wrong strategy quickly is another recipe for failure.

3.2.3 Strategy Definition – creating the 'big picture'

A well-defined strategy defines the overall target operating model required to achieve the aspirations in the strategy. It is this integrated 'big picture' that provides the map of where the organisation is going and

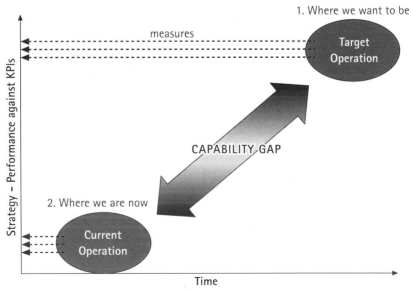

Figure 3.1 'Big picture' view – current and target operating models

what it will feel like for the employees and clients when they get there.

If the target operation represents 'where we want to get to' then the current operation must be assessed in the same terms in order to understand 'where we are now'.

3.2.4 Strategic planning

Having modelled the desired future state, strategic planning identifies the set of actions required to migrate from the current operation to the target operation. This is the crucial test of the feasibility of the strategy. There may need to be a number of iterations; reworking the strategy and plans until a challenging but credible outcome is achieved. The resulting strategic plan

- describes how the 'target operation' will be achieved through a coordinated set of projects
- is supported by a refocusing of operational plans (see figure 3.2).

If the language of 'required capabilities' is used then auditable links can be maintained between the strategy and the projects required to deliver

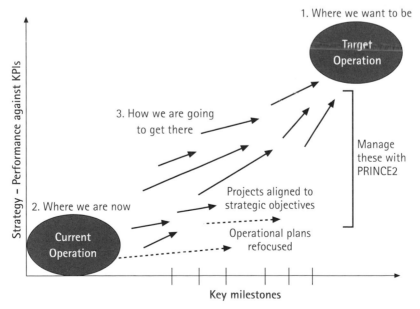

Figure 3.2 'Big picture' view – strategic plan

strategic objectives. In a controlled Project Environment there is a clear focus on the delivery of these capabilities via project deliverables. A key principle of PRINCE2 is the focus on products or outcomes rather than activity. When applied in the operation these products provide new capabilities (e.g. radically improved client service via the Internet).

The planning activity needs to be informed by a real understanding of the organisation's ability and capacity to change. A common approach is to use the numbers and skill levels of a core group of people as an indicator (e.g. project managers, IT professionals). A more comprehensive set of indicators is available only when the organisation manages its projects in a controlled and disciplined environment, such as PRINCE2, in which past performance can be understood.

There are two critical areas to be considered for successful integrated planning:

Project Environment

- The ability of the organisation to deliver the new capabilities needed in the timescales required
- The ability to manage non-strategic projects in a way that minimises disruption to the strategic change agenda and aligns their deliveries with the target operating model.

Operational Capability

- The ability to accommodate change in the operation and exploit new capabilities to achieve strategic benefits
- The ability to refocus existing capabilities to align with the organisation's strategic plan.

These capabilities are explored in more detail later in this section.

3.2.5 Aligning operational plans and change programme plans with strategy

The big picture view provides a powerful mechanism for understanding how activities must be aligned and resources coordinated to ensure that the organisation moves in the right direction at the right speed. The key issue is balancing the needs of the 'business as usual' operation with the

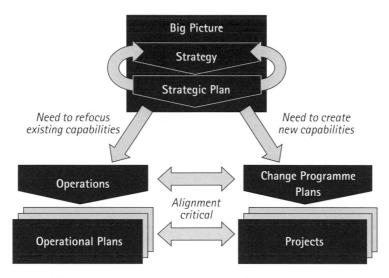

Figure 3.3 Aligning operations and projects with strategy

need for strategic change. Figure 3.3 illustrates the close alignment required.

Alignment with strategy can only be maintained through 'joined-up management' and a disciplined approach to managing change. If strategy is loosely connected or just expressed as an ambiguous set of aspirations, the organisation will struggle to do the right thing in projects and in the operation. In this situation people attempt to fill the vacuum with their own interpretation of where the organisation should be going, which at best wastes resources and at worst moves the organisation in the wrong direction.

When strategic alignment is working, each project will have its scope clearly set in terms of the capabilities it will deliver across the different elements of the operating model (e.g. product and service propositions, business processes, organisation structures, people, systems and infra-structure). In effect the definition of these capabilities constitutes a clear statement of the benefits of each project. One of the key tenets of PRINCE2 is the tight definition of project scope and verification at the end of every stage that the scope is still the same and also still valid. This approach, teamed with

15

- a clear business case underpinning every project
- involvement of the top team in sponsoring and directing the project and in key decisions
- inclusion of operations people (users) and suppliers in defining and directing the project and in 'gateways' between stages

constitutes the kind of integrated management approach that optimises control and the chance of success.

3.2.6 Managing the portfolio of strategic and non-strategic projects

In the real world an organisation's change agenda does not consist only of the well structured set of strategic projects that has been defined by the top-down planning process. Strategic planning and the subsequent management of the overall portfolio of change need to acknowledge the other projects which will run in parallel with strategic projects.

These might include changes to respond to new legislation, incremental operational improvements or routine renewal of infrastructure. Most organisations wish to do more than they have the resources to deliver so resources need to target the areas of greatest return on investment. To achieve this a clear process is needed to develop a business case for each proposed change. The parameters set by PRINCE2 mean each business case is constructed to the same rules and effective prioritisation is possible.

3.2.7 Moving into Strategy Implementation

This section has described how Strategy Definition should determine the right set of projects to achieve the organisation's strategy. The next describes the critical success factors for Strategy Implementation, focusing on what constitutes an effective Project Environment.

3.3 The Project Environment

The critical success factors for implementing strategic change and realising the benefits are

- an effective Project Environment as the key tool for the delivery of the organisation's plans
- sound Operational Capability to deliver the day-to-day business.

Operational Capability	Project Environment
• Ability to deliver the organisation's business as usual efficiently and effectively.	• Ability to deliver the new capabilities the organisation needs efficiently and effectively.
• Client outcomes being achieved consistently well.	• Ability to mobilise highly motivated cross-functional teams to deliver full solutions.
• Effective operational management and control mechanisms in place.	• Effective project management and coordination mechanisms in place.
• Deployment of existing capabilities fully aligned with strategic objectives.	• Project deliveries aligned with strategic objectives.

Figure 3.4 Critical success factors for effective strategic change

For organisations to achieve maximum benefit from strategic change they must excel in the management of both day-to-day operations and projects. Figure 3.4 shows the two sets of capabilities that must be balanced and aligned. This balance is critical as illustrated by the following scenarios:

3.3.1 Operational capability without an effective Project Environment

- Power lies mainly in the current operation
- Change is resisted
- People see no benefit in taking part in projects
- Change is seen as an externally driven event
- Projects fail to engage the key stakeholders on whom benefits realisation depends
- Implementation of change is painful and difficult
- Projects fail.

Organisations at this end of the spectrum might include long established companies operating in traditionally stable markets, public sector bodies which have not been restructured for many years, or organisations which have never regarded change as a core discipline (and may have always farmed out major changes to external suppliers and/or consultants).

3.3.2 Good Project Environment but no effective Operational Capability

- Change is imposed on a submissive operation
- People in the operation are collectively unable to articulate their requirements
- Operational impacts of changes are not understood, solution designs are fatally flawed
- Changes delivered by projects don't stick because there is no effective process management in the operation
- Benefits are not realised.

Examples of organisations fitting this description might include start-up companies who have continued with a dominant project mentality or organisations which have been subjected to radical restructuring (e.g. acquisition or merger) for whom a stable business operation has yet to be re-established.

3.3.3 Neither a good Project Environment nor an effective Operational Capability

Organisations without either of these competencies are probably incapable of strategic change and living on borrowed time.

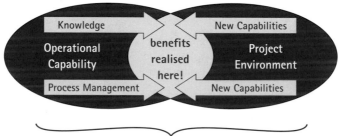

Deployment of key resources balanced across operations and projects

Figure 3.5 Operational Capability and project culture fully aligned

3.3.4 The winning formula – Project Environment, Operational Capability and alignment between the two

Organisations with the right balance and alignment between Operational Capability and Project Environment are well placed to achieve their strategic ambitions. This winning scenario can be characterised as follows:

- Change is seen as 'business as usual'
- Operational people feel that they have a stake in the projects being undertaken (i.e., 'It's being done by us, not to us')
- Project people feel they have a stake in the success of the changed operation they are delivering (i.e. 'We will be operating this after implementation')
- People who can facilitate cross-functional working are highly valued
- People move easily between Operational and Project domains
- The focus is on outcomes and benefits realisation
- Change to the operation is smooth and is scheduled to minimise disruption
- Redesigned business processes are implemented into a well-managed operational environment in which compliance with the new working practices can be monitored
- Projects and Operations agree about how benefits will be realised and by whom
- Operations start the process of benefits realisation early, in the confidence that new capabilities will be delivered as planned (e.g. allowing natural wastage of staff in areas where headcount reductions will be possible once new systems are delivered)
- Operational knowledge is fed effectively into projects at the right times (e.g. requirements definition, business process design, acceptance testing).

3.3.5 Critical elements of an effective Project Environment – overview

Having established the key dependency on the organisation's Operational Capability, what constitutes an effective Project Environment can

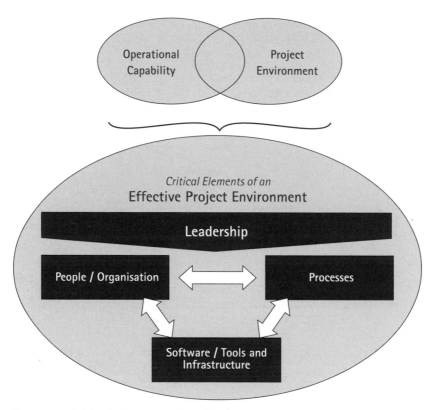

Figure 3.6 Critical elements of an effective Project Environment

now be set out in detail and the benefits of PRINCE2 illustrated in this context.

As figure 3.6 illustrates, an effective Project Environment depends on

- the right project **processes**
- being performed by the right **people**
- deployed within the right **organisational** structures
- supported by the right **software** tools and **infrastructure**
- in the context of clear top-down **leadership** providing the discipline to conduct projects consistently in the right way.

If any one of these elements is weak or missing then an effective Project Environment cannot be said to be in place.

The next sections take each element in turn, describing why it is critical, identifying its key attributes and indicating where and how PRINCE2 delivers against each one.

3.3.6 Leadership

An effective Project Environment can only be sustained if there is clear leadership from the top of the organisation. It is critical that everyone understands what attitudes and behaviours are most valued by senior management. The objective is to achieve real focus, alignment and discipline; harnessing people's energy to achieve maximum benefit; and taking friction and wasted time out of the change process. PRINCE2's evolution and best practice status is totally congruent with this objective. It sets the pattern for behaviour from top to bottom within the project.

This leadership is critical within the organisation, and it also communicates an important message about the organisation's change capability to stakeholders, clients and strategic partners (current and potential). It will build confidence in the organisation's ability to anticipate and respond to whatever opportunities and threats emerge in the environment it operates in. Benefits will accrue in terms of the ongoing support and investment of stakeholders and increased propensity of other players to partner with the organisation.

To provide the leadership required the senior team need to show a real understanding of why the Project Environment is critical and the controlled environment is necessary. Their consistent message should emphasise the constancy of change and the need to master it, underlining the role of the Project Environment in this process. The organisation will reap benefits in the following ways if the message hits home:

- ability to implement change quickly and efficiently
- ability to coordinate a complex change portfolio
- smooth implementation into the operational environment
- ability to continuously improve our change process
- flexibility in deploying resources across projects
- ability to all 'speak the same language' in describing projects

21

- ability to work as one team regardless of functional boundaries
- ability to monitor and measure in a consistent way and make the right decisions on prioritisation and commitment of resources.

These key messages are best communicated by a combination of formal rules and a set of Executive attitudes and behaviours that help create the environment within which the principles embodied by the rules will be applied.

Rules

This should not be a bureaucratic rule book but between four and six high-level statements that make the expected set of behaviours quite clear. For example

'No project moves beyond feasibility without a Project Initiation Document formally approved by the Project Board'

This clear set of rules must be visible and acted upon throughout the organisation. They should be set in the context of an overall environment that ensure they are universally perceived as common sense. It is not enough for projects to pay lip service to the use of a particular project management methodology but an environment should be established where everyone abides by the basic rules without question. Creative energies should focus on the business issues at hand rather than on debating the relative merits of different project management approaches.

It is important that these rules are seen to emanate from the senior management rather than from the organisation's specialist project management group (or one department which may have been early adopters of formal project management disciplines).

The senior team's attitudes and behaviours

The ways in which the senior management team can build an effective Project Environment vary from organisation to organisation. Typically, however, these actions and attitudes make a real difference:

- Communicate a clear statement of intent that all significant change must be managed within the controlled Project Environment
- Acknowledge and reward the champions of change within the organisation

- Endorse the informal community of project managers and support their development through PRINCE2 training
- Demonstrate the importance of the project management principles and rules through own behaviour (e.g. no exceptions for pet projects). PRINCE2 will reinforce the desired behaviour as, for example, projects can only be progressed where they have a sound business justification
- Actively engage in resolving project issues quickly if they have correctly been escalated to Executive level
- Support and empower the people who take the initiative to establish cross-functional mechanisms and lines of communication. PRINCE2 enables senior management to manage by exception and therefore to delegate much of the day-to-day control of the project with confidence
- Welcome real messages about project progress and issues; never shoot the messenger; encourage transparency and openness
- Be seen to be living the Project Environment, take part in project events and communications, visiting and contributing to projects (i.e. not just 'royal visits')
- Adopt the common language of the Project Environment and insist on its use whenever appropriate
- Actively monitor formal reporting against project Key Performance Indicators. PRINCE2 uses the Project Board as a key mechanism for reporting that allows senior management to have clear visibility of the project progress and issues and therefore the control that is required
- Operations management actively engaging in projects; encouraging and rewarding the contribution of their people to project success
- Demonstrate and encourage cross-functional behaviour
- Give equal weight to project needs and operational and/or functional needs when deciding on resource allocation
- Sustain a feeling of energy and excitement around the change agenda

ipport and encourage internal communications regarding
iccessful projects

- Manage the balance between all elements of the Project
Environment, investing in the people, process and tool elements
as appropriate, as failure to manage the balance can cause a
project to lose focus and veer off track.

3.3.7 Processes

Project Management processes represent
what is actually done in practice, how the
organisation defines, initiates and executes
projects. They are the real backbone of an
effective Project Environment and should
embody the high-level rules and principles being communicated by the
senior management in their leadership of the Project Environment.
PRINCE2 provides senior management with the conditions that they
need to provide effective leadership through the clear definition of the
senior management role and responsibilities and of the processes and
organisation required. For example, the role of the Project Board allows
the senior managers of the principal and partner organisations to work
collaboratively and truly understand the progress of the project, and to
make effective decisions based on accurate and timely information.

A good set of project management processes will consistently achieve
predictable and measurable outcomes. It is important that each project
management process is understood in the following terms:

- What is its overall **objective**?
- Who are its key **stakeholders**?
- What **outcomes** does each stakeholder need from the process?
- How will we **measure** that each outcome has been achieved?
- What **outputs and/or products** will achieve each outcome?
- What **quality criteria** should be applied to each output?
- What **activities** are needed to produce these outputs?
- What **resources** are required to carry out the activities?

- What knowledge and other **inputs** are required?
- What is the role and responsibility of senior management?

By asking and answering the above questions not only at the outset but at every stage or progress point throughout the project, PRINCE2 ensures that the objective remains in focus at all times. Each process should be defined and communicated in such a way that it is quite clear what is expected each time the process is carried out.

Formal process management disciplines should be applied to the project processes. These include explicit process ownership, performance measurement and mechanisms for continuous improvement such as process mapping and re-engineering. This will ensure that processes do not ossify and that they reflect the times and current technology. New practices or changes from the accepted practice should still be sanctioned and assessed via pilot exercises rather than by renegade projects unilaterally deciding to do things differently.

There is real benefit in the community of project managers taking a leading role in the ongoing development of project management processes, regardless of whether project managers are drawn from a single specialist group or a virtual pool from around the organisation. By monitoring and recording projects' performance of project processes the strategic planning function can build a realistic view of the organisation's change capability and inform the estimating of costs and benefits for future projects.

The need for a formal project management approach

In order to make the process

- repeatable
- predictable
- managed
- measurable and
- controllable

a set of managed materials defining the task breakdowns, products, and roles that make up the process is necessary. These templates and route maps should represent the collective experience of the organisation in running projects, reflecting best practice built up over the years. Ideally they should be accompanied by a user's guide explaining when some elements must be used, and recommending the optional use of others, guiding staff towards the best way to achieve all the required outcomes of the project process.

Many organisations short-cut the creation of this knowledge base by adopting PRINCE2 which is itself best practice and can provide the core for the organisation's project management processes. Section 3.4 describes in detail how PRINCE2 does this.

To summarise the case for pursuing project management and, in particular, PRINCE2:

Benefits of a formal project management approach

- Creation of a 'common language' to improve communication
- Consistent execution of project processes
- Reduction in non-value added time in and around projects
- Projects can concentrate on the business issues at hand rather than reinventing project processes.

Additional benefits of adopting a market leading non-proprietary approach

Organisations are increasingly involved in change initiatives that go beyond their own boundaries, within the context of alliances and partnerships. Because PRINCE2 is a market-leading approach the following additional benefits accrue and the organisation is able to

- engage external resources (e.g. contractors, new employees) who already 'speak the language', understand what is required, and can therefore become productive members of the team quickly
- partner with other organisations in joint ventures with reduced friction and faster collaborative working
- select third party suppliers to execute projects on the organisation's behalf without sacrificing the benefits of the established Project Environment
- benchmark externally and drive up performance.

3.3.8 People and organisation

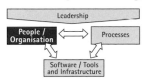

An effective Project Environment ultimately consists of a critical mass of people with the right skills, attitudes and behaviours. These are not just the people working in project teams, but also those in operations, functional specialists and people in all other parts of the organisation. It is a mistake to neglect the 'people' part of the equation in favour of project management methodologies and tools. This can happen because the 'soft' people issues are seen as more difficult and time consuming. It is not enough for the senior management to endorse a set of project management principles and invest in project management processes and tools; they also need to create an extended team of people who are prepared to 'live' the Project Environment. The challenge of strategic change demands positive attitudes and energy around the change agenda, both within projects and across the whole organisation.

This section considers the issues relating to individuals within the Project Environment (**People**) and then goes on to examine the context that must be created for them to work in (**Organisation**).

People

It is critical that the Project Environment lives in the hearts and minds of the individuals within the organisation. The quality of a change capability is embodied in the individuals within operational and project domains in step with the strategic aims of the organisation. This can only be achieved through the alignment, competency, and attitudes of individuals and their project management skills.

These are examples of the skills and behaviours that should be highly valued:

- people who contribute to projects with both discipline and common sense, channelling their energy and enthusiasm through the agreed processes
- people who are fully focused on *project* objectives but are at the same time sensitive to *operational* needs
- people who are fully focused on *operational* objectives but are at the same time supportive of *project* imperatives

27

- people who can facilitate cross-functional working
- people who build their careers through success in both operational and project roles
- people on projects who apply project management disciplines at all times regardless of their own role (i.e. not leaving these disciplines to be externally applied by the people in 'project manager' or 'Project Office' roles)
- specialists who can communicate and work effectively with others (rather than adopting a defensive attitude of 'knowledge is power')
- people on projects who take the initiative in managing relationships with the project's stakeholders.

To achieve this the mechanisms for aligning people's behaviour must be correctly tuned, for example:

Career paths

In organisations without a real Project Environment, stepping out of an operational role to join a project can turn out to be a bad career move. The individual can be out of sight and out of mind as far as career progression is concerned, or worse still may find that there is no operational role to go back to when the project is finished.

Talented people should be encouraged to move between operational and project roles and their career progression should match the value they add in both domains. It is in the organisation's interest to have people who understand both projects and operations. The incentives should be in place to encourage this, ideally reinforced by high-profile role models.

Recognition and rewards

In a healthy Project Environment success in operational and project roles is equally weighted and performance management processes fairly assess the contributions people make in both arenas. Furthermore, the rewards and recognition for people who have stepped out of a role in order to take on a challenge in a project should match both the contribution they have made and the risk they have taken in leaving the 'comfort zone'.

Professional development

Support for formal training and accreditation in project management disciplines can provide an important statement of intent for the organisation. This should not be confined to a specialist group of project managers but should be extended to all people who could have a significant bearing on the success of projects in different roles (e.g. Project Board Member – Executive, Senior User and Senior Supplier – and project manager). To encourage mobility between operational areas and projects, as recommended above, operational managers are key candidates for project management training. PRINCE2 provides users with an extensive range of training and consultancy services to assist with the mapping of a project management career path and the training and accreditation of the team.

Organisation

The way projects are organised and configured to interact with the rest of the organisation can make an important contribution to the overall Project Environment. This section first considers organisation in and around individual projects, then the wider structures that make up the environment within which projects operate.

How individual projects are organised

The organisation of each individual project must reflect the alignment between it and its key stakeholders; in particular the operational areas where project benefits will be realised. The project must not be a closed entity (except where the need for confidentiality overrides this). PRINCE2 emphasises transparency and communication with the rest of the organisation, providing for this by ensuring effective communication: both the 'customer' and the 'supplier' are represented on the Project Board. The principle of a 'customer' and 'supplier' is central to the PRINCE2 approach, promoting control through the formal definition and agreement of a 'contract' between the two parties.

Communication mechanisms

Effective two-way communication between the project and the wider organisation is important. This could be achieved through a number of mechanisms including open project rooms, open days, brainstorm and

29

review, 'Post-it note' sessions and touring road shows as well as the more conventional bulletins in newsletters or on the Intranet.

The objective is to allow the project to benefit from the collective knowledge of the whole organisation as well as to promote preparedness and anticipation in the community affected by the changes.

In addition to this broad campaign to raise awareness and readiness, targeted and formally managed activities should communicate with specific stakeholders of the project (areas and individuals within areas). There may be specific relationship objectives defined for individual stakeholders and people within the project are specifically accountable for achieving these objectives. The aim is to keep significant areas and individuals 'inside the tent' so that the project can succeed.

Figure 3.7 illustrates this set of relationships between the project and its stakeholders.

3.3.9 The overall Project Environment

In addition to the positive ways in which individual projects can be configured, there are a number of factors relating to the overall environment within which projects take place that can contribute to the right Project Environment. Examples include:

- an environment where it is natural for operational areas to lend good people to projects. This is easier where the project management approach is widely known and used
- fluidity in the way people move from project to operational roles and vice versa
- a vigorous informal community of project management people enabling continuous improvement of the resource pool and communication of best practice
- project roles understood and valued (e.g. Senior User and project manager)
- formal ownership of project management processes
- acceptance of the guiding project principles which are applied without heavy bureaucracy, and are not seen as being imposed from outside by project management specialists
- people across the organisation do not just pay lip service to the rules of the Project Environment

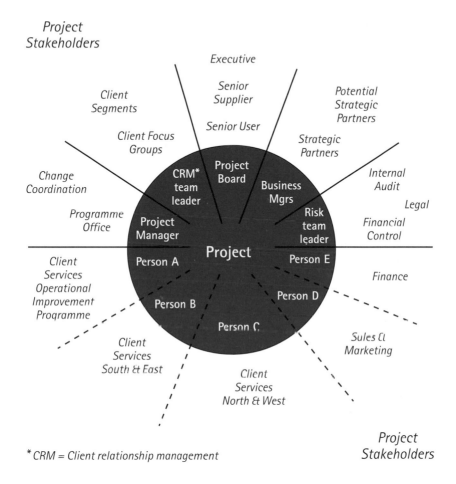

*Project
Stakeholders*

Executive

Senior
Supplier

*Client
Segments*

*Potential
Strategic
Partners*

*Client Focus
Groups*

Senior User

*Strategic
Partners*

*Change
Coordination*

CRM*
team
leader

Project
Board

Business
Mgrs

*Internal
Audit*

Legal

*Programme
Office*

Project
Manager

Risk
team
leader

*Financial
Control*

Project

*Client
Services
Operational
Improvement
Programme*

Person A

Person E

Finance

Person B

Person D

*Client
Services
South & East*

Person C

*Sales &
Marketing*

*Client
Services
North & West*

*Project
Stakeholders*

* *CRM = Client relationship management*

Figure 3.7 Mapping of project stakeholder management roles

- people genuinely understand the required outcomes of project processes rather than following a task list without really appreciating the purpose
- an overall confidence and self-belief in the organisation's own Project Environment (i.e. it is not undermined by external suppliers proposing to bring in their own project management method).

3.3.10 Software tools and infrastructure

Having the right tools and infrastructure significantly improves the chances of an effective Project Environment being sustained. Some might argue that for larger organisations the necessary consistency and control is not possible without significant automation of project processes and communication mechanisms. Nevertheless, tools in particular need to be selected and applied with focus and discipline so that they truly enable project processes (rather than forcing the use of practices inconsistent with the Project Environment). In the diagram used throughout this section it is significant that 'software tools and infrastructure' is shown at the bottom, with a supporting role in relation to 'people/organisation' and 'processes'. It would be a mistake to try to build the Project Environment by starting with the selection of a set of software tools. Only when the required project processes are in place, being performed by people with the right attitudes and behaviours, are the conditions right for tools to be introduced in a disciplined way to support what they are trying to achieve.

Case study 3.1

A company invested in three different project management toolsets in five years, each time hoping that use of the new toolset would create a consistent and disciplined Project Environment. Eventually it was accepted that the issue was the culture into which the tools were being introduced and this was addressed in a top-down manner.

The right software tools and infrastructure can, however, make a significant contribution to the Project Environment.

3.3.11 Software tools

There is a long history of mainframe and PC based tools that support project planning and resource scheduling and techniques like Critical Path Analysis. Careful use of these is clearly beneficial provided the information is not confined to the computer screen and detailed reports. It is often more important to have large visible diagrams that groups of people can debate and understand together, even if some of the intricate detail is not visible. Carrying out slick automatic task rescheduling on a PC package does not in itself realign large numbers of people with a change in plans.

Other well established uses of software tools include

- shared project repositories with support for document version control and/or configuration management
- enabling of project processes through groupware (e.g. Lotus Notes)
- hypertext-style automation of project management methodology documentation (e.g. PRINCE2 CD ROM documentation)
- communication of project status information via Intranet.

More recent innovations include

- use of an integrated project and/or operational knowledge base for impact analysis, scenario testing etc.
- collaborative working across organisational boundaries using Internet technologies.

'Low-tech' tools

Whilst new technologies always seem to offer the hope of breakthrough improvements in productivity and quality, it is often the case that simpler tools are better suited to the sort of Project Environment described in this section:

- brown paper and 'Post-it' notes to enable fast, collaborative brainstorming of project task dependencies
- project schedules on large posters
- big charts showing the deliverables for a project team, with spaces to tick completed stages.

3.3.12 Infrastructure

Project accommodation and equipment can also reinforce the principles of the Project Environment in a number of ways. These are over and above the normal hygiene factors of decent working spaces and facilities. Examples include:

- project 'war rooms' with key progress information all around the walls, where people come together to monitor progress and manage issues
- project communication area with open door policy
- mock-up of the future operational environment; the people who will use the new facility to be delivered by the project can come here and see simulations of what it will be like
- space allocated to the project for large-scale brainstorming and communication sessions
- communication infrastructure to support efficient collaborative working between dispersed groups (e.g. videoconferencing).

Appropriate use of these types of facilities can deliver significant benefits but may also incur significant cost. Therefore making provision for them is tangible proof of an organisation's commitment to the Project Environment.

3.4 How PRINCE2 supports the creation of an effective Project Environment

Figure 3.8 illustrates graphically how PRINCE2 covers all the key components that make up the controlled Project Environment, thus providing an effective approach to project management and a foundation for the management and delivery of successful change.

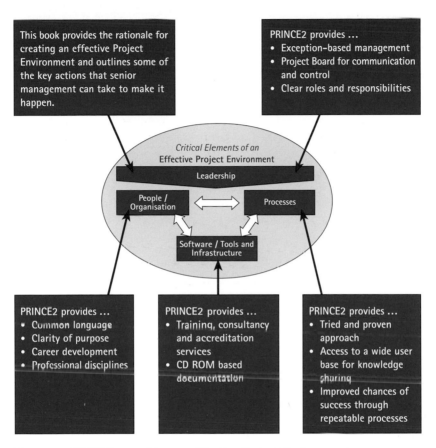

Figure 3.8 PRINCE2 provides an effective Project Environment

4
PRINCE2

The previous chapter summarised the role of projects and controlled environments in translating strategy into meaningful actions. This included an overview of PRINCE2 as a proven project management approach. This chapter identifies how PRINCE2 facilitates the delivery of projects within controlled environments and describes the benefits.

4.1 Overview

PRINCE2's key principle is its focus on deliverables, or products rather than activity, to create a better environment in which to control a project's likely outcome. Product or deliverable-based planning is a well-established project management technique. The products and outcomes are clearly defined at the outset and the dependencies between them are mapped, allowing the project to remain focused on achieving business results, whatever the current activity.

The checks, balances and results focus of PRINCE2 contributes to the control necessary to accommodate the inevitable changes to the original plan without invalidating the purpose or scope of the project. PRINCE2 recognises that changes to the original plan will occur and provides processes for dealing with these changes. Change, whether voluntary or involuntary, can have a huge impact on the success of a project and needs to be carefully monitored and managed to ensure the scope and output remain appropriate to the business case: changes which are missed or ignored can have a catastrophic impact. PRINCE2 deals with the unexpected by ensuring that

- procedures are in place for issues to be surfaced early and closed appropriately
- the business case for the project and the specification of changes required are baselined and that changes to the original business case are only approved if the appropriate control processes are followed.

The method provides a phased approach to the project and allows for a number of review points. These review points, usually after each stage of the project, allow for the original justification for the project to be scrutinised and reaffirmed or adjusted as circumstances dictate. The key benefit for senior management is that the project needs to clear these control hurdles if it is to continue to the next stage. A project unable to justify the move to the next stage may be closed. Senior management therefore have control to direct the project and are well positioned to ensure that the planned benefits (original or adjusted) continue to justify the project.

Poor risk management is an area of historic weakness in change projects. PRINCE2 provides processes for risk identification, analysis and mitigation planning. The approach ensures that risks are visible throughout the life of the project, and that any change in the status of these risks is understood early enough to allow sufficient time for management to assess the potential implications and initiate appropriate countermeasures.

Clear roles and responsibilities are key if the project processes outlined are to be executed effectively. PRINCE2 provides a model of the organisational requirements and in particular focuses on the roles and responsibilities of senior management. In PRINCE2, senior management controls the project through the Project Board which owns the project and is responsible for delivery of benefits and controlling costs. Since the Project Board reflects the stakeholders in the project, any decisions or changes to the baselined plan in terms of costs, time or specification are endorsed by it, scope for the unexpected is minimised and all parties remain 'onside' with each decision.

4.2 Processes and components

PRINCE2 comprises a set of generic, universal processes that should underpin any well managed project. The intensity with which each of these processes is undertaken can be varied according to project circumstances or particular organisational needs. However, the principle is that if each process is applied properly the scope for loss of control, unexpected deviation from the objectives, and surprises, is minimised.

A key concept of PRINCE2 is that it clearly differentiates between

- the management of the development process, and
- the development process itself.

This is an important benefit as it allows the organisation to focus on the change it needs to make and not waste valuable effort on understanding the project management process for delivering it. Through the use of the common PRINCE2 terminology, the organisation can avoid fruitless debate about, for example, the precise definition and content of a business case. It is far more valuable that the organisation uses its energy and resources to understand the precise nature of the business change in the context of its own business and the design of the solution delivered by the change.

PRINCE2 is constructed around a process-based approach to project management. The processes clearly define the management activities to be carried out during the life of the project. Additionally, a number of project management components, which are applied at appropriate points in the processes, are also described.

Figure 4.1 shows the major project management processes and the components that underpin them. Together these processes and components provide the building blocks for a controlled and therefore effective project management environment.

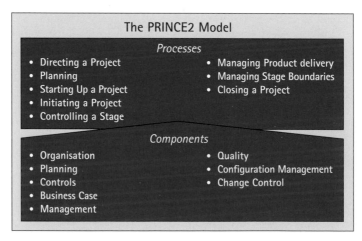

Figure 4.1 PRINCE2 processes and components

The project processes and components ensure that

- there is an effective linkage between strategy and Strategy Implementation, where the strategy is described as a balanced set of measurable targets that, when achieved, will deliver an improved operational model. Projects mobilise the related activity and deliverables into a portfolio of actions
- the goals of a project can be reviewed and adjusted in light of experience
- there is a 'big picture' to support Executive decisions regarding resource allocation and reallocation
- the impact of changes can be assessed and decisions in response to these changes ensure that the organisation's resources remain optimised and targeted at the desired benefits
- activity can be organised allowing for effective delegation of management
- risks are continually identified and assessed allowing for effective mitigation strategies for each to be developed and tracked
- issues surface early and are therefore more likely to be managed optimally
- communication to all stakeholders is timely, accurate and targeted at the appropriate audience
- the benefits are understood and are kept visible for the duration
- the critical path through a complex set of activities and deliverables can be described simply, tracked and adjusted as dictated by changes in the original drivers of the project.

4.2.1 The processes

PRINCE2 defines eight processes for the effective management of a project.

Figure 4.2. shows the broad relationship between the eight processes within PRINCE2.

The diagram is a simplified view of the process model, as individual organisations will want to tailor it to meet their specific requirements. However, every project will need to apply each of the processes to some extent, to be determined at the initiation stage.

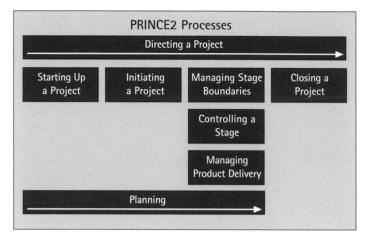

Figure 4.2 PRINCE2 processes

Each of the processes is now described, with references to the project components where appropriate. Particular attention is paid to those with specific interest for senior management.

Directing a Project

This process provides the senior management responsible for the project and its outcomes with the means to direct the project's resources. *Directing a Project* is effectively a decision making process. A key principle of PRINCE2 is that senior management should be able to manage the project on an exception basis. This reduces the time that senior management need to commit to the project but that there is not the loss of control that is sometimes seen as a benefit of using a more 'hands-on' approach.

The process covers the whole duration of the project from start-up to closure and has five major activities:

1 Authorising the development of a business case and project plan
2 Approval for the project to commence
3 Checking that the project is still justifiable at key interim review points
4 Monitoring progress and providing direction

5   Ensuring that the project comes to a controlled close and that lessons and experiences are learned for the benefit of future projects.

Directing a Project is an important process, as it acts as a filter to ensure that the organisation is not wasting resources on the development of proposals that will never make the starting line: a 'pet project' will probably lack a clear business justification and consequently will struggle to develop a compelling business case, for example. These non-runners need to be sifted out as often the resources most skilled in defining a business case are scarce and senior management need to know they are developing business cases that have some probability of proceeding.

As already outlined, PRINCE2's Project Board is the organisation of the senior management and group responsible for the project, including the sponsor, the senior business owner responsible for the delivery of the benefits and a senior representative of a supplier organisation. As such it is the principal forum for directing a project, effectively the decision making body charged with all approvals of changes to the original business case. The exact design of the Project Board should dovetail with the organisation's reporting framework. As figure 4.3 suggests, however, the reporting process for projects should be separate from that used for 'business as usual' reporting to set aside sufficient time and attention to understand the project's status and allow the Board to provide an effective steer for the project team.

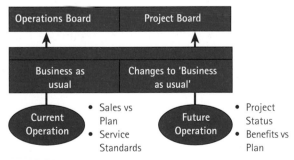

Figure 4.3 The Project Board

Starting Up a Project

This is generally a short process when compared with the duration of the overall life of the project and it has four primary objectives:

1   Clarify and communicate the aims and benefits of the project
2   Design and appoint the project management team
3   Decide on the approach the project will take to deliver the required solution
4   Plan the work needed to draw up the 'contract' between customer and supplier.

Initiating a Project

Initiating a Project prepares the business case for the project. The business case will determine whether the project can justifiably proceed when compared with other candidate projects or against agreed relevant criteria (time, technology, budget). The business case is described in a formal document called the Project Initiation Document (PID). This document is baselined and any changes to the project have to be assessed against it to determine whether the project is still justified. The PID is also the control mechanism that allows the project's progress to be monitored. Ultimately the project's success will be measured against the original objectives of time, cost and quality as defined in the PID.

The PID would normally include the following:

- Business objectives – a clear articulation of the strategic objectives to which the project has been aligned to deliver
- Critical success factors – the benefits which, when delivered, will determine the success of the project
- Key Performance Indicators – the measures and targets used to test the achievement of benefits
- Impacts – the key business impact of the changes, both internal and external
- Assumptions – the critical going-in assumptions that have been made
- Constraints – what constraints have been set that limit the approach?
- Dependencies – what are the things the project requires from others and by when? Also, what do they require from the project?
- Options evaluation – a precise summary of the options evaluated and the criteria for weighting them

- Recommended option – define the scope of the delivery in terms of
  - product or service improvements
  - distribution
  - geographic locations
  - business processes
  - organisational coverage
  - systems and technology
  - specific scope exclusions
- Financial evaluation – the business case for the project in the form of a cost-benefit analysis
- Benefits analysis – a detailed analysis of the benefits described in the Financial Evaluation. Ideally this should comprise:
  - a description of each change that will deliver a specific benefit
  - the measure that will be used to determine success
  - the new performance target for the change
  - the person who will provide the measure
  - the level of confidence attached to achieving the revised performance
  - the owner of the benefit, usually an individual
  - the basis for calculating the benefits to be derived from the new performance target
- Delivery plan – the general approach to be taken including
  - a clear milestone plan showing the key deliverables, their timing and dependencies on others both within and outside the project
  - product breakdown structure and product descriptions showing the precise design of the deliverables and their dependencies
- Project costs – to include both the costs of delivery (the one-off costs) and the post-implementation costs of live running (the ongoing costs)
- Risks and issues – the key risks and issues facing the programme and the owner along with actions to deal with them

- Resource plan – the resource requirements and phasing of the resources required to deliver the project. This would include a description of specific skills required.

A careful and considered project initiation is crucial to a successful outcome because the costs of the project are described and committed at this stage. Many projects fail due to a poorly executed project initiation stage so senior management have to be confident that the business case is a true reflection of the likely project costs and benefits. Figure 4.4 shows the relationship between project phases and the extent to which costs are committed at any given point.

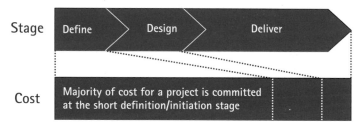

Figure 4.4 The majority of cost is committed during the relatively short project definition/initiation stage

Organisations should resist the temptation to move from definition to design too quickly. All too often there is pressure to move from initiation or definition to design driven by the flawed belief that this will demonstrate that a project is making progress. The problem that this approach presents is that the design can be based on fundamentally flawed understanding of the real costs of delivering the planned business benefits.

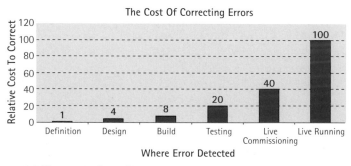

Figure 4.5 The cost of quality

44

To illustrate this, figure 4.5 shows the relative costs associated with correcting errors at a range of points in the project lifecycle. It highlights very clearly the imperative for a robust initiation and design as the cost of correcting an error identified in live running is 100 times the cost of correcting an error identified in the definition phase.

The following example of a recent project, case study 4.1, highlights the problems associated when a flawed design has resulted from an unclear initiation process.

Case study 4.1

A major UK bank developed a new capability based on a flawed business case. As the objectives of the project were unclear from the outset the project ran massively over budget in terms of time and cost and the deliverable was regarded as being very poor quality.

The bank is now constrained by a poor design and cannot implement its business plan for the new capability.

PRINCE2's rigorous requirements in the earliest stages of a project minimise scope for jumping the gun or starting work with incomplete information or justification.

Controlling a Stage

A key principle for controlling a project is to break the whole into a number of manageable stages. These stages afford a number of important control points for the senior management team to review the ongoing justification for the project and decide whether it should be allowed to proceed into the next stage. This approach is of particular benefit where a project has a lengthy duration. In addition, subdivision can help motivate the team as the review points allow them to see light at the end of the tunnel at the end of each stage and their efforts can be recognised at these stages. This phasing also encourages the early release of benefits; it avoids having all benefits planned for delivery at the end of a project and therefore prone to accumulated risk and delay.

PRINCE2's *Controlling a Stage* process describes the monitoring and control activities required to keep a stage on track by providing the information required to allow the anticipation of, and response to, any changes to the business specification or to the status of the project risks.

This is a core process for the project manager and makes up the majority of the day-to-day activity of PRINCE2 project management.

Managing Product Delivery

Managing Product Delivery produces a contract between the project and the specialists who will produce deliverables. This contract is particularly important where work is being outsourced to a third party supplier. PRINCE2 calls the work agreed in this process a 'work package'. It covers details about schedules, quality and reporting requirements. The primary benefit of this approach is that it removes the chances of there being any ambiguity between parties as to what is required by whom and by when. This clarity is possible as all partners in the project are using the common language of PRINCE2.

Managing Stage Boundaries

As described earlier, the project is more manageable and provides greater control for senior management if it is chunked into stages. The key business benefit of this is that senior management can decide if the project is still justified at a number of points in the project lifecycle. Managing Stage Boundaries facilitates

- planning the next stage of the project
- updating of the project plan
- updating of the business case
- updating of the risk assessment
- reporting on the outcome and performance of the stage just completed
- approval from senior management to move into the next stage.

Planning

Planning is an ongoing process throughout the project. To avoid wasted time and effort PRINCE2 stipulates that detailed planning is only carried out for the next stage to be undertaken. This allows the experience of the current and preceding stages to inform the planning of the next stage. This type of planning process supports PRINCE2's product-based approach. The planning process aims to

- design the plan
- define and analyse the plan's products or outcomes
- identify the necessary activities to produce the products or outcomes
- identify the dependencies between the products and the activities to produce them
- schedule the resources
- analyse the risks
- describe the planning assumptions and quality steps.

Planning must be pragmatic and constructed to provide a summary of the project to senior management and a more detailed view to allow the project manager to manage resources at a more local level. Typically, project managers will require a level of plan that allows them to manage activity on a weekly basis. PRINCE2 encourages pragmatic planning and thus avoids the trap that many organisations fall into of planning in too much detail too far into the future. Case study 4.2 illustrates the problems of poor planning.

Case study 4.2

An insurance company entered into a partnership with a major software provider. The objective for the project was highly ambitious and early estimates indicated that the project would use several hundred staff for a two-year period. The third party had limited knowledge of the business but were allowed to manage the project. The chief project planner undertook to produce the plan and was soon floundering in too much detail. The initial plan presented to senior management took three months to produce. It was bound in a folder two inches thick. There was no summary available. The plan was so complex it was estimated that it would take three weeks to produce the weekly summary.

Six months into the project there was still no credible plan available. The company decided that the planning fiasco was a clear indication that the provider had inadequate control of the project and the contract was terminated.

Closing a Project

Closing a Project is important because it provides for the accumulation of best practice in project management for use by future projects. It covers the activity required to close a project at its planned end or at an earlier date if so directed by senior management. The objectives are to

- record the extent to which the objectives set out at the start of the project have been met
- confirm the customer's satisfaction with products and benefits
- confirm that the maintenance and support arrangements for the products are in place
- recommend any follow-up actions
- ensure that lessons learned from the project are communicated to improve processes for future projects.

4.2.2 The components

Some of the components of PRINCE2 have been covered at a high level in the above description of the project processes, for example, Planning and Organisation. A further component, the Management of Risk, is now considered in terms of its relevance for senior management.

Management of Risk

Risk is of particular interest to senior management and calls for careful consideration during the project lifecycle. Risks are defined at the outset of the project and can be viewed from two perspectives – risk probability and risk severity. Risk probability is a measure of the likelihood of a future event or situation negatively impacting the project. Risk severity measures the anticipated damage of the impact should the risk actually occur (become an Issue).

There are four key steps for managing risks

- identification
- evaluation
- development of a risk plan
- monitoring the risks and maintaining the risk plan.

The use of risk identification and evaluation checklists are core parts of

PRINCE2 and the project will use these best practices and templates to facilitate the risk management process. Typically the risks will be brainstormed out in a workshop involving all those who have a stake in the project. The following list gives some examples. The use of the checklist ensures that no potential risk area is overlooked.

- Project size: numbers of staff, deliverables and budget
- The extent and use of new technology
- Project timescales, particularly where these are imposed, say for regulatory reasons
- Number of third party service providers involved
- Staff (skills and experience)
- The choice and use of project methodologies
- Project team location
- Track record of managing similar change.

The checklist will ask a number of questions to be answered regarding each risk to determine the probability of the risk becoming an Issue. The probability is rated as high, medium or low.

Risk probability assessment

Programme and project methodologies are
- well-established in the organisation ☐ Low
- established, but not fully practised ☐ Medium
- informal ☐ High

The example provided associates a low probability of risk if project methodologies are well established in the organisation, and a high probability if there were no formal approaches to project management in use. Once the project risks have been identified and their probability rated they can be assessed to determine the severity of the risk should it occur.

At this point in the risk management process it is possible to identify areas where the project is most exposed to risk, these being the areas where risks have a high probability and a high severity. A risk management plan can then be drawn up to deal with the risks.

The plan assesses each risk and proposes one of the following strategies

- transfer
- accept
- avoid
- reduce
- prepare a contingency plan.

To maintain the visibility of risks they are captured and maintained in a risk log. This log is a key component of the project reporting process to the senior team.

One of the success factors for effective risk management is the assignment of each risk to a clear owner whose responsibility it is to monitor the risk and who has the authority to make decisions to bring the risk to a resolution in the shortest possible time. Readers may like to refer to OGC's *Management of Risk: Guidance for Practitioners* (The Stationery Office Ltd, 2002) for details of best practice in risk management.

Impact of risk outside the project

It is clear that risk management within projects is close to the heart of senior management because the outcome in terms of deliverables and the impact on those involved will vary in line with the quality of the risk management.

Since projects are typically undertaken within larger frameworks of change such as programmes, the ultimate benefits and stakeholders of one project may be those of a whole range of projects within these programmes. As far as PRINCE2 is concerned, therefore, the management of both benefits and stakeholders falls within the discipline of programme rather than project management. Readers may like to refer to OGC's *Managing Successful Programmes* (The Stationery Office Ltd, 1999) for details of this best practice in programme management.

Change Control and Configuration Management

No project can be considered under control if it allows uncontrolled changes to what it was agreed that the project would deliver. Such changes can destroy cost, time, scope and quality control. PRINCE2's components include both change control and configuration management; protection and security for the project's products. The activities necessary for the effective working of these components is included seamlessly in the PRINCE2 processes.

Quality

Achieving the required quality of product (and the right quality of project management) is an essential feature of any project. Far too often a check on the quality of the final product(s) is left until one of the final steps of a project – with the resulting delays and expense until any failings are put right. This assumes that any quality flaws were not built into the product at specification or design time. Discovery of such quality flaws near the end of a project can be impossible to correct fully. PRINCE2 builds quality work into a project from the very outset and provides key events to assess throughout the project whether it is being achieved.

4.3 Why PRINCE2 works

There are several fundamental reasons why PRINCE2 works in almost all instances:

- because PRINCE2 is so widely used and has been developed from and into best practice, an organisation can adopt it and avoid the pitfalls associated with ad hoc approaches
- by using a consistent and repeatable set of processes the organisation can build up a valuable asset bank of project experiences
- resources can be moved freely between projects, thanks to the common language PRINCE2 brings to all projects
- the controlled start, controlled progress and controlled close allow the organisation to focus on the benefits it wants to achieve rather than unduly worrying over how it will deliver them
- the principle of management by exception means that this control does not come with an excessive cost in valuable senior management time
- management by exception allows senior management to delegate with confidence by setting parameters for project costs and time, allowing them to become involved at a detailed level only when the parameters are breached or when a high-level decision on project direction is required.

Summary

In summary, the key features and resulting benefits from PRINCE2 are that

- PRINCE2 works because it ensures through the development of a business case that the right projects are undertaken and that these are done right
- PRINCE2's delivery focused approach describes products or outcomes which are essentially the definition of the benefits the project will deliver. Understanding the project's products allows the organisation to map more easily the dependencies between them and the activities required to produce them
- PRINCE2 chunks the project into manageable stages. Although a high-level plan will be developed at the outset to support the business case, only at the end of each stage, when the business case is reviewed are detailed plans constructed for the next stage. This minimises the scope to waste resources on projects which are going to fail, be off-specification or become redundant
- PRINCE2 adopts a pragmatic approach to the management of project risks and changes to the baselined specification. Senior management perform the role of high-level decision maker, accommodated through the Project Board
- PRINCE2 is adaptable and will seamlessly dovetail with the individual requirements of any organisation. PRINCE2 is flexible in that it supports any type of project regardless of size
- PRINCE2 works because it ensures clear roles and responsibilities. Ownership of the definition and realisation of the benefits is clear from the outset.

Research and experience demonstrate that an organisation will greatly enhance its chances of successfully managing change when it adopts a proven, structured and controlled approach to project management such as PRINCE2.

PRINCE2 provides a ready-made solution, which provides a fast track to effective project management allowing the organisation to focus on exploiting the benefits that come from well-managed change.

Chapter 5 sets out the key lessons learned from the best practice process and shows how PRINCE2 can help organisations avoid repeating the mistakes of the past.

5
MANAGING PROJECTS – KEY LESSONS ADDRESSED BY PRINCE2

This book has advocated the need for a controlled environment for the successful management of change. This conclusion has been drawn from extensive research and actual examples from both the public and private sectors. This chapter summarises the key lessons drawn from that research and the best practice gathering for PRINCE2 and indicates how PRINCE2 can help organisations achieve successful and sustainable change.

5.1 Project Environment

To achieve a radical step-change in business performance an organisation needs to develop an integrated and controlled approach to the definition and delivery of its corporate aspirations. We have described the solution as a Project Environment, which gathers into a single framework all the required elements that collectively provide the conditions needed to drive organisational success. We have discussed the need for a cultural revolution where the solution to managing business changes is not to simply purchase a 'solution' and hope that it succeeds. There is a real need for the top team to champion the Project Environment and lead the organisation on a journey that many may find quite alien from existing practices. The key lesson for senior management is that they must grasp control of the current environment and through skilful and enthusiastic leadership implement the Project Environment in such a way that others willingly follow. Each organisation will need to decide for itself how best to implement this new capability; however, PRINCE2 can provide the fast track to dramatic increases in business performance through its boldness of attack and a radical approach to implementation.

5.2 Leadership

Coordinating all the aspects of change requires effective leadership and that is only possible where the responsibility for the project falls to a senior member of the management team. If responsibility it is not clear at the outset, then it is almost impossible for a project to succeed.

In PRINCE2 clear processes are defined for the involvement of each member of the project. This includes definitions of their roles and responsibilities. The organisation for the project is defined and particular attention is given to the role of the senior managers. The Project Board ensures that business ownership is clear for all to see and that the business has tight control over the project. Because key stakeholders are involved and engaged throughout the whole of the project they determine the level of quality for each deliverable. Through the guidance provided by the key stakeholders the project is focused on delivering solutions that are fit for purpose and are not over-engineered, as is often the case where new technology is being used.

5.3 A formal approach to project management

Although there are many reasons for project failure the reasons can be grouped broadly as 'management' and 'technical'.

By far the greatest cause for failure lies in the management group and is usually the use of an ad hoc approach to the task, which rarely provides the controlled environment that successful change management requires.

PRINCE2 fosters the controlled environment that minimises opportunities for unexpected deviation from scope, budget, specification or schedule.

5.4 The scope of change

Traditionally, organisations have concentrated on only one element of change, often the IT element. For successful change management, an approach is required that allows for all aspects of the change and its impact to be considered.

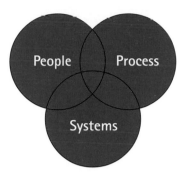

Figure 5.1 Change must manage the impact on all aspects of the operation

PRINCE2's framework of tried and tested processes enables organisa-tions to mobilise teams of specialists from various business functions. Effective cross-functional working is a key benefit of a formal project management approach.

5.5 Improve project management skills

Good leaders who have a clear responsibility for change are not sufficient by themselves. Good management needs to permeate the whole organi-sation. The leader will need a team that is able to deliver. The delivery of change is a challenging task and highly skilled and experienced project workers are vital to success.

PRINCE2 project management processes allow for a repeatable appli-cation of these skills. As a common language is used, the resources can be moved from project to project and the knowledge and experience from each is developed and grown to become a key company asset. The increase in capability for the organisation can be measured through the formal examination and accreditation of staff within PRINCE2's training and professional development structure.

5.6 Greater focus on risks

Focusing on the delivery of business benefits requires a greater awareness of the potential risks to the organisation of project failure. There are specific actions within project management that need to be taken in the area of risk management.

Within PRINCE2 risk management is defined as a key management process. The four steps of effective risk management are described in detail, these being

- Identification
- Evaluation
- Development of a risk plan
- Monitoring the risks and maintaining the risk plan.

Project risks are identified at the outset and actively tracked and managed for the duration of the project. Risks are rated in terms of their probability and impact and recorded on a formal risk log. Each risk is assigned an owner who is responsible for monitoring the risk and the implementation of mitigating plans to address them. The risks and the status of the actions to contain them are made visible at a senior management level by the risk log being an integral part of the reporting process.

5.7 Manageable chunks

Managing the risk of project failure can be made easier if ambitious and complex projects are broken up into manageable chunks. This chunking will also help to keep the team motivated as they can see the light at the end of the tunnel. This approach also avoids the pitfall of one big delivery at the end of the project.

At the heart of PRINCE2 is a phased approach to planning which allows for the project's initial justification to be reviewed at various key points. The phased approach also allows for pragmatic planning where only the next phase of a project is planned in detail, resulting in less wasted time on detailed planning at the outset and replanning along the way.

5.8 Define, track and measure quality

Projects need to manage expectations by defining early on what the benefits are, what constitutes 'fitness for purpose' (quality) and by setting out how the benefits will be realised.

Figure 5.2 describes the three key variables of a project – time, cost and quality (benefits).

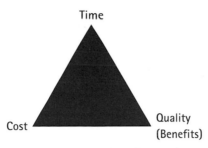

Figure 5.2 The three key project variables of cost, time and quality or benefits

These three variables describe a project simply and make up the structure of a business case. Beyond the definition of the business case any change to one of these variables will have an impact on one of the other variables. Each variable will need to be measured to construct the business case.

- **Time** is the simplest to measure. A common method for its measurement exists and all understand it
- **Cost** of a project is the next easiest to measure, although many organisations have a poor track record. However, every organisation should have a finance capability that can be developed to track and control the costs (and benefits) associated with the project
- Measuring **quality** or **benefits** is the most difficult. In particular, measuring realised benefits is impossible if they have not been defined at the outset with clear performance targets that can be tracked back to improvements in the current operation.

PRINCE2 uses a product- or outcome-based approach to project management. The techniques provided allow for the benefits of the project to be modelled clearly, and the time and cost to produce them understood.

5.9 Improve supplier relationships

Often, the change agenda cannot be delivered by the organisation alone. Suppliers have a major role to play, and implementing an improved approach to managing change will be impossible if relationships with suppliers or procurement are poor.

PRINCE2 has the concept of a supplier-customer relationship at its very core. Through this attitude the project can draw up formal contracts for the work that a supplier will undertake and the deliverables to be provided. PRINCE2 recommends that the supplier organisation also adopt PRINCE2 to enable effective cross-company working with both organisations using the same language.

The Project Board ensures that key stakeholders, including third party suppliers, are appropriately involved in the decision making process.

5.10 Develop project management skills

The current change agenda places a huge demand on organisations and suppliers to expand the skills that they will need to deliver successful business change. A fundamental element of good management (of anything, not just of change projects) is enabling lessons to be learned and knowledge and experience to be shared, for example, through peer review and good practice gathering.

PRINCE2 users have access to a wide range of suppliers for both the method and the training and development services. Users of PRINCE2 can achieve an external accreditation, which provides recognition of their skills. As a common language is used throughout an organisation the experiences and knowledge gained from projects can be shared more easily than if an ad hoc approach is used.

PRINCE2 provides the environment for organisational learning, too, as the processes are repeatable and therefore the overall improvement in the organisational capability to deliver successful change can be measured.

Summary

PRINCE2 offers the tried and tested processes and organisation that make up an effective Project Environment. This provides senior management with the pragmatic and controlled environment that is a prerequisite for the successful management of change.

Through adopting PRINCE2, organisations can access a fast track to the skills and set-up that will enable them to manage change well and deliver business benefits through project management.

6
GLOSSARY

Acceptance Criteria

A prioritised list of criteria that the final product(s) must meet before the customer will accept them; a measurable definition of what must be done for the final product to be acceptable to the customer. They should be defined as part of the Project Brief and agreed between customer and supplier no later than the project initiation stage. They should be documented in the Project Initiation Document.

Activity network

A flow diagram showing the activities of a plan and their interdependencies. The network shows each activity's duration, earliest start and finish times, latest start and finish times and float. Also known as 'planning network'. See also Critical path.

Baseline

A snapshot; a position or situation that is recorded. Although the position may be updated later, the baseline remains unchanged and available as a reminder of the original state and as a comparison against the current position. Products that have passed their quality checks and are approved are baselined products. Anything 'baselined' should be under version control in configuration management and 'frozen', i.e. no changes to that version are allowed.

Benefits

The positive outcomes, quantified or unquantified, that a project is being undertaken to deliver, and that justify the investment.

Benefits realisation

The practice of ensuring that the outcome of a project produces the projected benefits claimed in the Business Case.

Business Case

Information that describes the justification for setting up and continuing a PRINCE2 project. It provides the reasons (and answers the question 'Why?') for the project. It is updated at key points throughout the project.

Change authority

A group to which the Project Board may delegate responsibility for the consideration of requests for change. The change authority is given a budget and can approve changes within that budget.

Change budget

The money allocated to the change authority to be spent on authorised requests for change.

Change control

The procedure to ensure that the processing of all Project Issues is controlled, including the submission, analysis and decision making.

Checkpoint

A team-level, time-driven review of progress, usually involving a meeting.

Checkpoint Report

A progress report of the information gathered at a checkpoint meeting, which is given by a team to the Project Manager and provides reporting data as defined in the Work Package.

Communication Plan

Part of the Project Initiation Document describing how the project's stakeholders and interested parties will be kept informed during the project.

Concession

An Off-Specification that is accepted by the Project Board without corrective action.

Configuration audit

A comparison of the latest version number and status of all products shown in the configuration library records against the information held by the product authors.

Configuration management

A discipline, normally supported by software tools, that gives management precise control over its assets (for example, the products of a project), covering planning, identification, control, status accounting and verification of the products.

Configuration status account

A report on the status of products. The required products can be specified by identifier or the part of the project in which they were developed.

Contingency budget

The amount of money required to implement a contingency plan. If the Project Board approves a contingency plan, it would normally set aside a contingency budget, which would only be called upon if the contingency plan had to be implemented.

Contingency plan

A plan that provides an outline of decisions and measures to be taken if defined circumstances, outside the control of a PRINCE2 project, should occur.

Critical path

This is the line connecting the start of a planning network with the final activity in that network through those activities with the smallest float. Often this is a line through the network connecting those activities with a zero float, i.e. those activities where any delay will delay the time of the entire network.

Customer

The person or group who commissioned the work and will benefit from the end results.

Deliverable

An item that the project has to create as part of the requirements. It may be part of the final outcome or an intermediate element on which one or more subsequent deliverables are dependent. According to the type of project, another name for a deliverable is 'product'.

End Project Report

A report given by the Project Manager to the Project Board, that confirms the hand-over of all products and provides an updated Business Case and an assessment of how well the project has done against its Project Initiation Document.

End stage assessment

The review by the Project Board and Project Manager of the End Stage Report to decide whether to approve the next Stage Plan (unless the last stage has now been completed). According to the size and criticality of the project, the review may be formal or informal. The approval to proceed should be documented as an important management product.

End Stage Report

A report given by the Project Manager to the Project Board at the end of each management stage of the project. This provides information about the project performance during the stage and the project status at stage end.

Exception

A situation where it can be forecast that there will be a deviation beyond the tolerance levels agreed between Project Manager and Project Board (or between Project Board and corporate or programme management, or between a Team Manager and the Project Manager).

Exception assessment

This is a meeting of the Project Board to approve (or reject) an Exception Plan.

Exception Plan

This is a plan that often follows an Exception Report. For a Stage Plan exception, it covers the period from the present to the end of the current stage. If the exception were at a project level, the Project Plan would be replaced.

Exception Report

A report that describes an exception, provides an analysis and options for the way forward and identifies a recommended option. The Project Manager presents it to the Project Board.

Executive

The single individual with overall responsibility for ensuring that a project or programme meets its objectives and delivers the projected benefits. This individual should ensure that the project or programme maintains its business focus, that it has clear authority and that the work, including risks, is actively managed. The chairperson of the Project Board, representing the customer and owner of the Business Case.

Feasibility study

A feasibility study is an early study of a problem to assess if a solution is feasible. The study will normally scope the problem, identify and explore a number of solutions and make a recommendation on what action to take. Part of the work in developing options is to calculate an outline Business Case for each as one aspect of comparison.

Follow-on Action Recommendations

A report that can be used as input to the process of creating a Business

Case/Project Mandate for any follow-on PRINCE2 project and for recording any follow-on instructions covering incomplete products or outstanding issues. It also sets out proposals for post-project review of the project's products.

Gantt chart

This is a diagram of a plan's activities against a time background, showing start and end times and resources required.

Gate review

A generic term, rather than a PRINCE2 term, meaning a point at the end of a stage or phase where a decision is made whether to continue with the project. In PRINCE2 this would equate to an end stage assessment.

Highlight Report

Report from the Project Manager to the Project Board on a time-driven frequency on stage progress.

Issue Log

A log of all Project Issues including requests for change raised during the project, showing details of each issue, its evaluation, what decisions about it have been made and its current status.

Lessons Learned Report

A report that describes the lessons learned in undertaking the project and that includes statistics from the quality control of the project's management products. It is approved by the Project Board and then held centrally for the benefit of future projects.

Off-Specification

Something that should be provided by the project, but currently is not (or is forecast not to be) provided. This might be a missing product or a product not meeting its specification.

Outcome

The term used to describe the totality of what the project is set up to deliver, consisting of all the specialist products. For example, this could be an installed computer system with trained staff to use it, backed up by new working practices and documentation, a refurbished and equipped building with all the staff moved in and working, or it could be a new product launched with a recruited and trained sales and support team in place.

Peer review

Peer reviews are specific reviews of a project or any of its products where personnel from within the organisation and/or from other organisations carry out an independent assessment of the project. Peer reviews can be done at any point within a project but are often used at stage-end points.

Phase

A part, section or segment of a project, similar in meaning to a PRINCE2 stage. The key meaning of stage in PRINCE2 terms is the use of management stages, i.e. sections of the project to which the Project Board only commits one at a time. A phase might be more connected to a time slice, change of skills required or change of emphasis.

Post-implementation review

See Post-project review.

Post-project review

One or more reviews held after project closure to determine if the expected benefits have been obtained. Also known as post-implementation review.

PRINCE2

A method that supports some selected aspects of project management. The acronym stands for PRojects IN Controlled Environments.

PRINCE2 project

A project whose product(s) can be defined at its start sufficiently precisely so as to be measurable against predefined metrics and that is managed according to the PRINCE2 method.

Process

That which must be done to bring about a particular outcome, in terms of information to be gathered, decisions to be made and results that must be achieved.

Producer

This role represents the creator(s) of a product that is the subject of a quality review. Typically, it will be filled by the person who has produced the product or who has led the team responsible.

Product

Any input to or output from a project. PRINCE2 distinguishes between management products (which are produced as part of the management or quality processes of the project) and specialist products (which are those products that make up the final deliverable). A product may itself be a collection of other products.

Product-based planning

A three step diagrammatic technique leading to a comprehensive plan based on creation and delivery of required outputs. The technique considers prerequisite products, quality requirements and the dependencies between products.

Product Breakdown Structure

A hierarchy of all the products to be produced during a plan.

Product Checklist

A list of the major products of a plan, plus key dates in their delivery.

Product Description

A description of a product's purpose, composition, derivation and quality criteria. It is produced at planning time, as soon as the need for the product is identified.

Product Flow Diagram

A diagram showing the sequence of production and interdependencies of the products listed in a Product Breakdown Structure.

Programme

A portfolio of projects selected, planned and managed in a co-ordinated way.

Project

A temporary organisation that is created for the purpose of delivering one or more business products according to a specified Business Case.

Project Assurance

The Project Board's responsibilities to assure itself that the project is being conducted correctly.

Project Brief

A description of what the project is to do; a refined and extended version of the Project Mandate, which has been agreed by the Project Board and which is input to project initiation.

Project closure notification

Advice from the Project Board to inform the host location that the project resources can be disbanded and support services, such as space, equipment and access, demobilised.

Project closure recommendation

Notification prepared by the Project Manager for the Project Board to send (when the board is satisfied that the project can be closed) to any organisation that has supplied facilities to the project.

Project Initiation Document (PID)

A logical document which brings together the key information needed to start the project on a sound basis and to convey that information to all concerned with the project.

Project Issue

A term used to cover either a general issue, query, a Request for Change, suggestion or Off-Specification raised during a project. Project Issues can be about anything to do with the project.

Project management

The planning, monitoring and control of all aspects of the project and the motivation of all those involved in it to achieve the project objectives on time and to the specified cost, quality and performance.

Project management team

A term to represent the entire management structure of Project Board, Project Manager, plus any Team Manager, Project Assurance and Project Support roles.

Project Manager

The person given the authority and responsibility to manage the project on a day-to-day basis to deliver the required products within the constraints agreed with the Project Board.

Project Mandate

Information created externally to the project, which forms the terms of reference and is used to start up the PRINCE2 project.

Project Plan

A high-level plan showing the major products of the project, when they will be delivered and at what cost. An initial Project Plan is presented as part of the Project Initiation Document. This is revised as information on actual progress appears. It is a major control document for the Project Board to measure actual progress against expectations.

Project Quality Plan

A plan defining the key quality criteria, quality control and audit processes to be applied to project management and specialist work in the PRINCE2 project. It will be part of the text in the Project Initiation Document.

Project records

A collection of all approved management, specialist and quality products and other material, which is necessary to provide an auditable record of the project.

NB This does not include working files.

Project start-up notification

Advice to the host location that the project is about to start and requesting any required Project Support services.

Project Support Office

A group set up to provide certain administrative services to the Project Manager. Often the group provides its services to many projects in parallel.

Quality

The totality of features and characteristics of a product or service that bear on its ability to satisfy stated and implied needs. Also defined as 'fitness for purpose' or 'conforms to requirements'.

Quality Management System

The complete set of quality standards, procedures and responsibilities for a site or organisation.

Quality review

A quality review is a quality checking technique with a specific structure, defined roles and procedure designed to ensure a product's completeness and adherence to standards. The participants are drawn from those with an interest in the product and those with the necessary skills to review its correctness. An example of the checks made by a quality review is 'Does the document match the quality criteria in the Product Description?'

Quality system

See Quality Management System.

Request for Change

A means of proposing a modification to the current specification of a product. It is one type of Project Issue.

Reviewer

A person asked to review a product that is the subject of a quality review.

Risk Log

A document that provides identification, estimation, impact evaluation and countermeasures for all risks to the project. It should be created during the start-up of the project and developed during the life of the project. Also known as Risk Register.

Risk profile

A graphical representation of information normally found on the Risk Log.

Risk register

See Risk Log.

Senior Responsible Owner

This is not a PRINCE2 term, but is used in many organisations. Its equivalent in PRINCE2 terms would be the 'Executive' role.

Senior Supplier

The Project Board role that provides knowledge and experience of the main discipline(s) involved in the production of the project's deliverable(s). Represents the supplier(s) interests within the project and provides supplier resources.

Senior User

A member of the Project Board, accountable for ensuring that user needs are specified correctly and that the solution meets those needs.

Sponsor

Not a specific PRINCE2 role but often used to mean the major driving force of a project. May be the equivalent of Executive or corporate/programme management.

Stakeholders

Parties with an interest in the execution and outcome of a project. They would include business streams affected by or dependent on the outcome of a project.

Supplier

The group or groups responsible for the supply of the project's specialist products.

Team Manager

A role that may be employed by the Project Manager or a specifically appointed alternative person to manage the work of project team members.

Tolerance

The permissible deviation above and below a plan's estimate of time and cost without escalating the deviation to the next level of management. Separate tolerance figures should be given for time and cost. There may also be tolerance levels for quality, scope, benefit and risk. Tolerance is applied at project, stage and team levels.

User(s)

The person or group who will use the final deliverable(s) of the project.

Work Package

The set of information relevant to the creation of one or more products. It will contain the Product Description(s), details of any constraints on production such as time and cost, interfaces and confirmation of the agreement between the Project Manager and the person or Team Manager who is to implement the Work Package that the work can be done within the constraints.